Page 1: *The Southern Sea Gate (Porta di San Marco) and the octagonal Tower of Saint Nicholas, known as Bourtzi. View from the north.*

Page 4: *View of the Main Gate to the Castle of Methone, from Morosini bridge.*

Page 5: *Detail of the image 69. Relief plaque set into a wall, depicting Saint Mark's lion.*

© KAPON EDITIONS – PETROS THEMELIS, 2022
FIRST EDITION: SEPTEMBER 2022
ISBN 978-618-218-004-4

All rights reserved. No part of this publication may be reproduced or republished, wholly or in part, or in summary, paraphrase or adaptation, by mechanical or electronic means, by photocopying or recording, or by any other method, without the prior written permission of KAPON EDITIONS. Law 2121/1993 and the regulations of International Law applicable in Greece.

KAPON EDITIONS
23–27 Makriyanni str., 117 42 Athens, Greece,
Tel. 0030 210 9235098, 0030 210 9214 089

RACHEL'S BOOKSHOP
22 Ploutarchou str., 106 76 Athens, Greece,
Tel. 210 7241 442, 210 9210 983

www.kaponeditions.gr   e-mail: info@kaponeditions.gr

PETROS THEMELIS

METHONE

ANCIENT | MEDIEVAL | MODERN

Translated by DIMITRIOS DOUMAS

KAPON EDITIONS

CONTENTS

7
INTRODUCTION

10
FROM ANTIQUITY TO BYZANTIUM

19
MIDDLE AGES – VENETIAN RULE – OTTOMAN OCCUPATION

29
SECOND VENETIAN RULE

32
THE LIBERATION

40
THE CASTLE OF METHONE

60
MODERN METHONE

63
BIBLIOGRAPHY

INTRODUCTION

Ever since I first set foot in the blessed Messenian land, in 1963, as curator of antiquities of the then 7th Ephorate of Prehistoric and Classical Antiquities that was based in Olympia, of all my favourite places, Methone has captivated my heart. The Venetian castle (fig. 1) and the impressive wide-mouthed wells of the town (fig. 4), the delipidated Kapodistrian school that was about to fall apart at that time (figs. 2–3), the traditional dwellings of this serene, silent settlement, the few inhabitants, the close proximity to the sea, the view of Sapientza and the other islands on the horizon have left an indelible impression on me. This unbreakable bond with Methone has been determined by my acquaintance and friendship with Takis Demodos (de Modon) —his real surname was Konstantinopoulos—, a noble scholar of Methone who fervently loved his homeland, history and tradition. He was a student at the Kapodistrian primary school, where his father served as a teacher. Takis, whose sole weapon was his own pen and his almost passionate love for his birthplace, struggled to keep the image of the fortress, the settlement and its historical elements unblemished, and preserve the threatened material remains of the area's traditional folk and urban culture. As a columnist, he fought against ignorance, indifference, brutality and

1. Aerial view of the castle and the settlement of Methone, from the North.

the misconstrued notion of development that had been embraced and inconsiderately carried out since then by a good number of contractors, hoteliers, local agents and others. We joined our forces presenting a common front against abuse. His essential on-site presence, knowledge and ardour were supported by my limited executive power in the implementation of the provisions of the archaeological law. In 1966, having noticed the appalling preservation state of the crumbling Kapodistrian school, I proposed its expropriation and the relocation there of the small archaeological collection of Methone that was still housed in Bourtzi. My visits to Methone were frequent, as I had undertaken the restoration of the west tower of the southern Porta di San Marco, dating from 1411, the fortified gateway of the Venetian castle, and the octagonal tower of Saint Nicholas, known as Bourtzi (figs. 5–6). The project's supervisor was my friend, the architect-engineer Aias Vazirgiatzikis. Over the same period, I was offered the opportunity to bring to light during excavation at the village Pylla, to the northeast of Gialova, a cist grave that contained as grave goods black-figure vases, dating back to the 6th c. BC, thereby corroborating the presence of an archaic settlement.

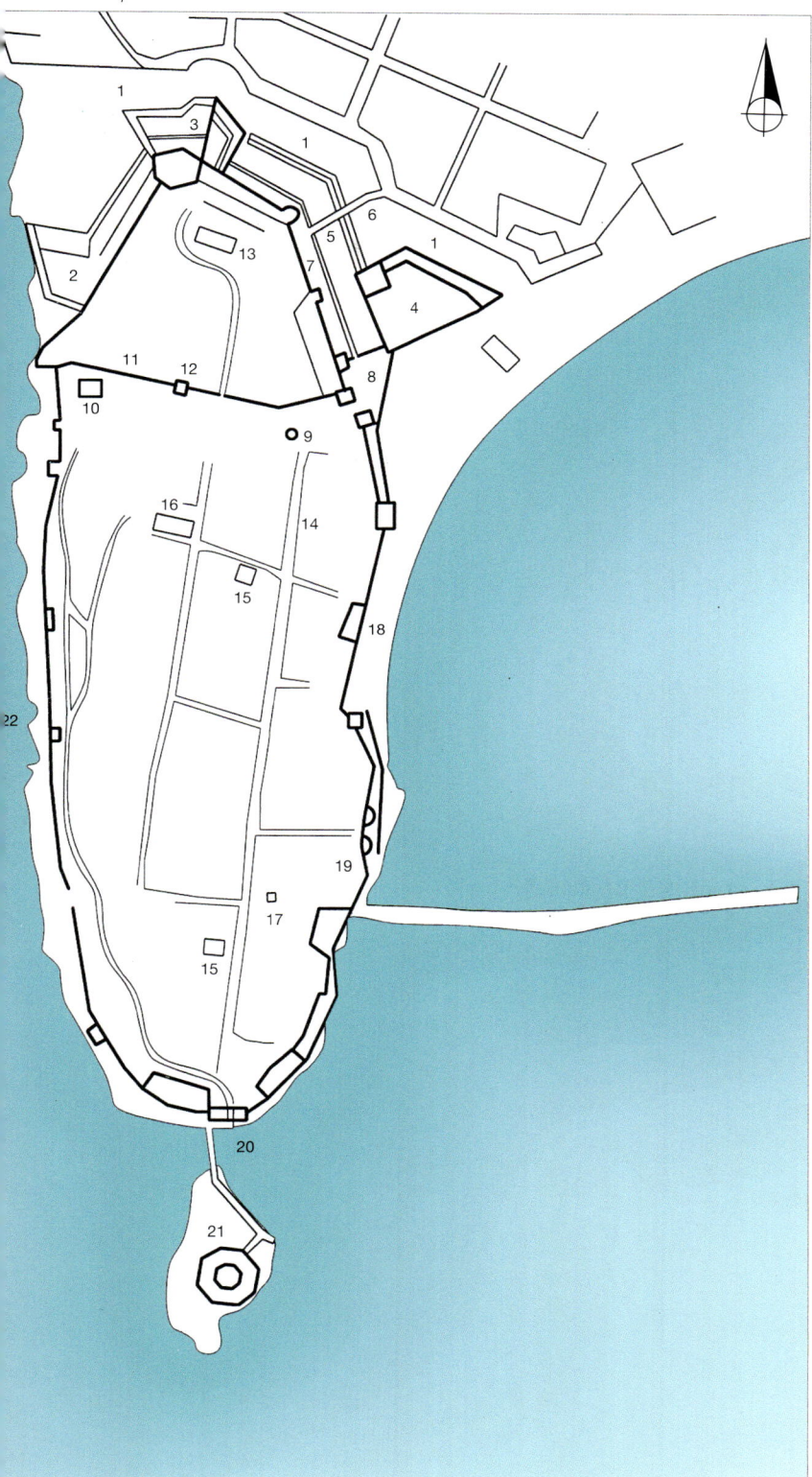

2. The facade of the Kapodistrian school of Methone, before restoration.

3. View of the Kapodistrian school of Methone, after the completion of restoration.

4. Venetian well at Methone.

5. View of the southern Porta di San Marco

6. The octagonal tower of Saint Nicholas, known as Bourtzi.

7. Topographic plan of the Fortress of Methone
1. *Great moat*
2. *Heliodysion*
3. *Bembo Bastion*
4. *Loredan Bastion*
5. *Main Gate*
6. *The bridge built by Maison*
7. *Entry corridor*
8. *Porta di Terra*
9. *Column of Morosini*
10. *Gunpowder magazine*
11. *Cross-wall*
12. *Gate to the citadel*
13. *Large gunpowder magazine*
14. *The main thoroughfare of the town*
15. *Ottoman baths* (hammam)
16. *Church of the Transfiguration of the Saviour*
17. *Remains of the church of Saint John the Theologian*
18. *Eastern gate (Porta Stoppa)*
19. *Gate to the harbour (Porta del Mandrachio)*
20. *The southern Sea Gate (Porta di San Marco)*
21. *Octagonal tower (Bourtzi)*
22. *West wall of the castle*

FROM ANTIQUITY TO BYZANTIUM

In 1996, on the Methone cove, at a relatively shallow depth, a settlement of the Middle Bronze Age (1900–1600 BC) was found submerged (fig. 8). However, it is questionable whether it was at that same place, or further to the northeast, where lay the Mycenaean and especially Homer's "vine-clad" Pedassos, one of the seven cities which Agamemnon had promised to offer as gifts to Achilles in exchange for the return of beautiful Briseis, who was violently taken away, according to the *Iliad* (Book 9, 152). The topographical problem is connected with the conflict between two men over a fair maiden, a mature

Mycenaean king, Agamemnon, and a haughty, invincible and irascible young warrior, Achilles, the son of the Nereid Thetis. Yet, the Homeric Pedasos was known to the historian Thucydides (2.25) as a "town of Laconia with its wall being weak", and the geographer Strabo (9.359.3) who makes a distinction between Methone in Messenia and the Macedonian city Methone, Eretria's colony in Pieria, that withstood a siege by Philipp II of Macedon during which he was seriously wounded in his eye. Thucydides recounts that when the Athenians and their allies were sailing around the coast of the Peloponnese in 431 BC, the first year of the Peloponnesian War, they landed at Methone, but failed to seize the city, as the Spartan general Brasidas happened to be in the district and repelled them.

Of particular interest is the information documented by Pausanias (4.18.1) according to which, following the First Messenian War in 700 BC, the only surviving part of Messenian territory —the so-called Koryphasion (figs. 9–10)— was retained by the people of ancient Pylos, who were still in control of the sea, and also by the neighbouring inhabitants of Methone. However, after the Second Messenian War, the peoples of Pylos and Methone were forced to abandon their cities and sought refuge in Cyllene, the coastal city of Elis (where lies today the medieval castle of Chlemoutsi and Glarentza, figs. 11–13), a significant port opposite the Ionian islands Zakynthos and Cephalonia (Paus. 4.23.1). When the territory of Messenia was finally captured, the Lacedaemonians installed in Methone the exiled Nauplians (Paus. 4.27.8). After the liberation of Messenia by the Thebans under Epaminondas, the Nauplians were left undisturbed by the repatriated men of Methone, because they maintained a sympathetic attitude towards them and had not sided with the Spartans.

With the onset of the Peloponnesian War in 431 BC, the Athenian general Carcinus, by order of Pericles, in an attempt to deceive the enemy, laid siege to the weak Methone with 150 vessels, 1,000 hoplites and 400 archers. However, as already mentioned, the conquest of the city was averted on account of the prompt intervention of the Spartan Brasidas who was involved shortly later, in 425 BC, in the military events at Pylos and Sphacteria (fig. 15) where he lost his shield during the battle against the Athenians.

In the wake of Messenia's liberation and the foundation of the capital Messene by the Theban general Epaminondas and his Argive allies, in 369 BC, Methone remained under Sparta's control, at least until 338 BC, the victory of Philipp II of Macedon at Chaeronea and his invasion of Laconia

8. Aerial photograph of the cove of Methone

9. *View of the fortified town of Koryphasion, from Voidokoilia Bay (copperplate engraving).*

10. *Aerial view of Koryphasion, west of the Lagoon (Divari) of Gialova.*

11

12

13

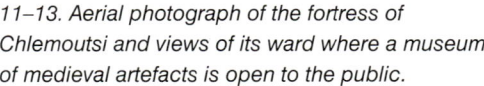

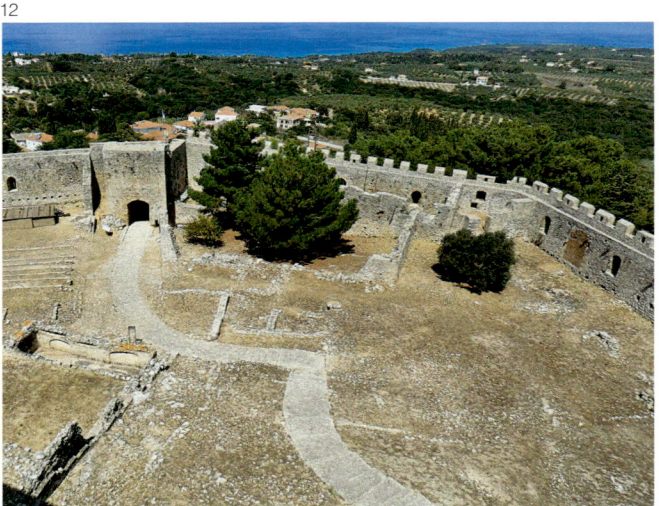

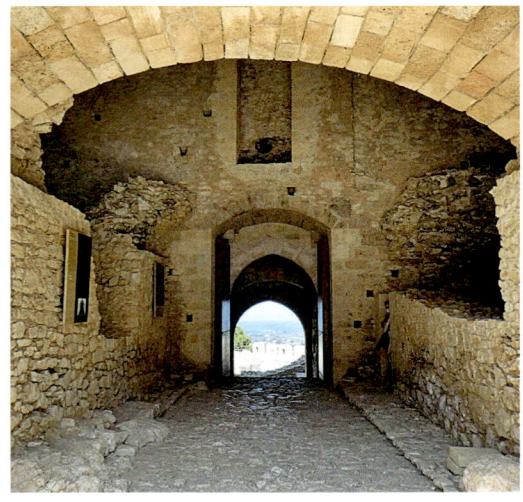

11–13. Aerial photograph of the fortress of Chlemoutsi and views of its ward where a museum of medieval artefacts is open to the public.

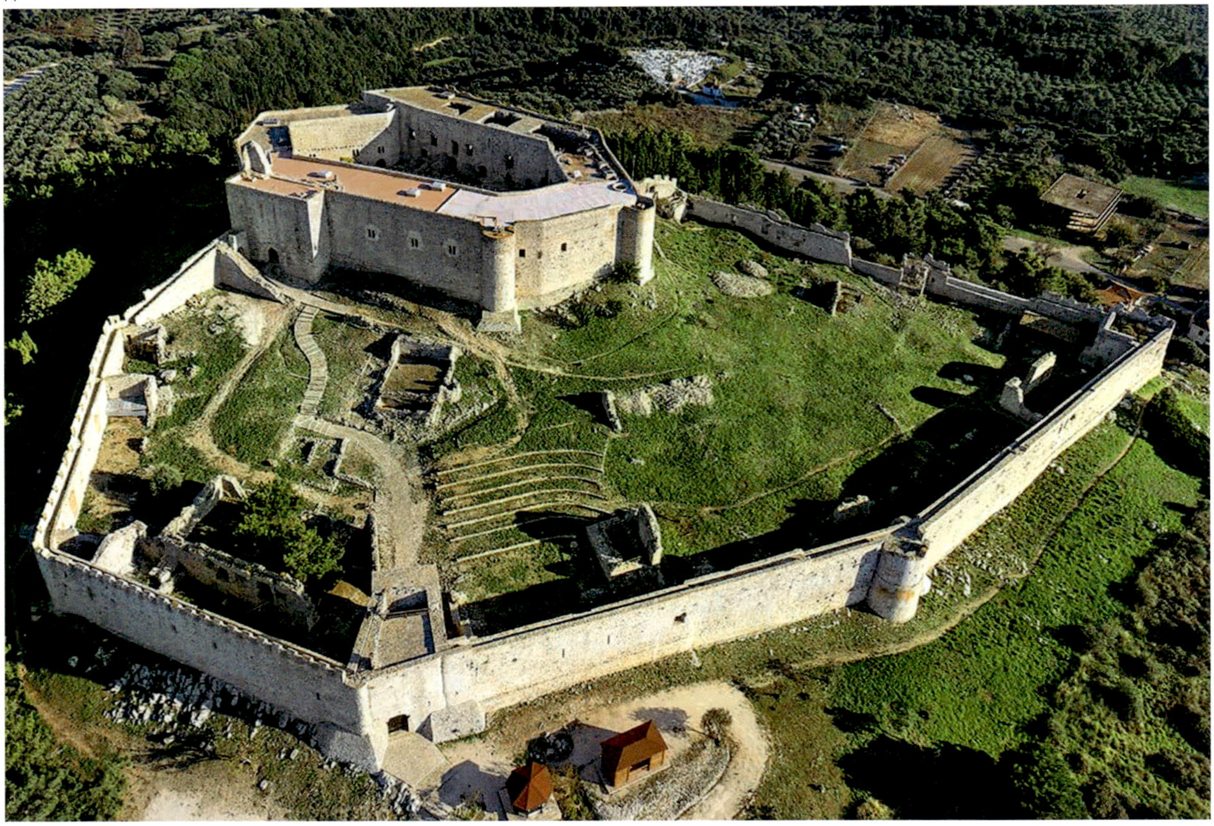

14. General view of the castle of Kalamata.

15. View of Sphacteria from the east. In the foreground are shown present-day Pylos and Niokastro.

immediately afterwards. The southern part of the Messenian territory, including Methone, Pylos, Pharae and Thuria, was at times under the control of Sparta that consistently laid claim to the border area of Dentheleatis on the south-western slopes of Mount Taygetos, to the northeast of Pharae, in present-day Kalamata (fig. 14).

Following the death of King Pyrrhus of Epirus and the end of his reign, the Illyrians, who lived in the region identified today with modern Albania, conquered Thesprotia and launched raids on the coast of Messenia. Pretending to be merchants, they anchored in Methone in 220 BC and purchased wine from the "vine-clad" city and traded "barbaric" objects attracting a large number of the population to the coast and then, by a surprise attack, they forcibly took away many of them —men and women— and carried them with their ships to Thesprotia leaving Methone almost desolate (Paus. 4.35.4–8).

In the momentous for the epoch conflict between the contenders of power in the Italian peninsula and the capital Rome, Octavian and Antony, lover and ally of Cleopatra, —a conflict whose outcome was determined at Actium, where Nicopolis, the Roman city of victory was established— the Messenians supported Antony and Cleopatra. The proficient general Marcus Vipsanius Agrippa (fig. 16), Octavian's son-in-law, besieged and conquered Methone in the spring of 31 BC, which until then was ruled on behalf of Antony by a small military force led by King Bogud of North Africa. From 31 BC onwards, Methone functioned as a significant station for the supply of Rome with grain from the granaries of Egypt.

Pausanias (4.35.3) who visited Methone during the reign of Emperor Antoninus Pius, in the 2nd c. AD, refers to a temple of Athena Anemotis (Subduer of the Winds), whose cult statue had been dedicated to the goddess by the Homeric hero Diomedes, according to the local tradition. This mythological tradition derives most likely from the fact that the Mycenaean king of Argos Diomedes, who had joined

16. Portrait bust of the Roman general Marcus Vipsanius Agrippa.

17–21. Architectural members of Greco-Roman antiquity coming from buildings of the ancient city of Methone-Mothone. Photos 17–19 by Panagiotis Foutakis.

Agamemnon offering 80 ships against Troy, was favoured by the goddess Athena, whereas one of his wondrous deeds was the taking of the Palladium from the temple of the goddess in Troy after the sack of the city. Moreover, some of the inhabitants of Methone were Nauplians, exiled from Argolis, as already mentioned, who evidently knew and admired the feats of their fellow countryman Diomedes. At the corner of the transverse street descending towards the Porta del Mandrachio or Dogana, lay the Ottoman mosque, built over the ruins of the temple of Athena. In 1828 the French soldiers of the commander-in-chief Nicolas Joseph Maison converted the building into a storage facility for the commissariat of the French expeditionary force. In fact, it is reported that, until 1830, some of the Ionic columns of Athena's temple were still visible.

At Methone, Pausanias also encountered the sanctuary of Artemis and a well that contained water mixed with pitch resembling in appearance the myrrh of Cyzicus, as he points out. The presence of pitch presupposes underground petroleum deposits (oil reserves have been discovered in the Ionian Sea); as for the comparison between the water found in the well and the famous "amarakion" myrrh of Cyzicus (see Dioscorides, 1.68, and Hesychius, s.v. amarakos), I believe that it is one of the traveller's numerous exaggerations.

In Roman coins minted at Methone between

20

21

the late 2nd and the early 3rd c. BC, are depicted the semi-circular harbour of the town and the cult statues of Athena Anemotis and Artemis, as well as other deities, such as Asclepius, Aphrodite and Tyche, which are not mentioned by Pausanias.

The surviving medieval fortification of Methone is built mostly of cast rubble faced with blocks of stone, some of which come from ancient fortifications, possibly of ancient Messene as well. In addition to the plain stone blocks, embedded into the wall are found scattered architectural members (column fragments, epistyles, column capitals) that belonged to buildings of the Hellenistic and the Roman period (figs. 18-21). It is possible that some of these members come from the ancient temples visited by Pausanias at Methone.

Stone stelae, pilasters and columns, recovered at the west stoa of the Gymnasium and the Palaestra of ancient Messene, are inscribed with catalogues recording the names of the ephebes of Messene, arranged into five groups corresponding to the five tribes (*phylae*) of the city (Aristomachis, Kleolaia, Hyllis, Kresphontis and Daiphontis) (figs. 22–23). In their majority, these catalogues date between 3 and 96 AD. In some of them, aside from the groups of ephebes of the five tribes and a sixth one that involves "Foreigners and Romans", added during the reign of Emperor Augustus, a seventh group of ephebes is included, under the title "those of the cities", documenting, in addition to those of the capital, ephebes of the towns of the Messenian territory, such as Mothonian, Asinian and Kyparisian residents. These towns are described as "those of the provinces", namely of the Messenian countryside. At the Gymnasium and the Stadium of ancient Messene, the youths studied for three years between the ages of 17 and 20, receiving education, also engaging in nude (*gymnikoi*) and equestrian (*hippikoi*) competitions (*agones*) and martial arts (fig. 24). Hence, Methone, despite the Illyrian invasion and the displacement of part of its population, was not deserted but continued to be inhabited and function institutionally during the Hellenistic period.

Nevertheless, this Messenian coastal town did not experience its heyday during the Classical and the Hellenistic period, nor during the Roman times when Emperor Trajan granted civic freedom and autonomy to the people of Methone ("*Μοθωναῖοις βασιλεύς Τραϊανός ἔδωκεν ἐλευθέρους ὄντας ἐν αὐτονομίᾳ πολιτεύεσθαι*"), disengaging them from the Messenian confederacy.

22–23. Catalogues of ephebes inscribed on pilasters and columns of the Gymnasium and the Palaestra of ancient Messene.

24. View of the Stadium – Gymnasium – Palaestra architectural complex of ancient Messene.

In the late 4th c. AD, Methone was devastated by a terrible earthquake that took place on July 6 366 AD and was felt across the entire Peloponnese, Crete, North Africa and Cyprus. According to the Roman historian Ammianus Marcellinus (330–392 AD), aside from the major disaster caused by the earthquake to cities (in Alexandria, for instance 10,000 people lost their lives), the losses of ships and among crew members were enormous. Marcellinus informs us that a Laconian vessel was found two miles away from the shore of Methone (A. Marcellinus, *Res Gestae* 17.46). Nonetheless, despite the earthquake, just twenty years later, the affluent patrician widow Paula, descendant of a powerful Roman family, together with her daughter Eustochium, spent a night at Methone on their pilgrimage by sea from Rome to the Holy Land, mainly Jerusalem.

Methone is referred to as episcopal see already since the 4th c. AD. As a byzantine town, it became known when in 533 AD Justinian signed a peace treaty with the Persians and sent his military commander Belisarius against the Vandals of North Africa who were based in Carthage. According to the narrative of the historian Procopius (Book 3, 13.9–10), when Belisarius set sail for Sicily heading towards Africa, he was forced to anchor his fleet in the harbour of Methone because of a storm. There he met his generals Valerian and Martinus, who had arrived in the area earlier (fig. 25). As the wind dropped, he disembarked his army and ordered that sea bread be baked in the local ovens since the loaves kept in the ships had become mouldy.

Many years later, in 881, Nasar, the admiral of the Byzantine fleet in the reign of Emperor Basil I (670–886), launched a sudden attack against a fleet of Saracen pirates that was anchored at Methone, and burned it destroying it completely.

25

MIDDLE AGES – VENETIAN RULE – OTTOMAN OCCUPATION

Six centuries later, in 1154, Methone is mentioned by the Arab Muhammad al-Idrisi in his *Geography* as a fortified city maintaining a naval force (fig. 26). Over the same period, the town provided asylum to a pirate squadron. Piracy that had already flourished for centuries across the Mediterranean and the Aegean Sea intensified in the reign of Emperor John II Komnenos, who abolished the privileges granted to the Venetians in 1082 by his father Alexios I, aiming to thwart the commercial and military infiltration of the Crusaders and the Western merchants into his state. The Venetians responded by sending their fleet to the Aegean devastating the islands and capturing women and children, whereas in 1125, Doge Domenico Michieli (1117–1130), known as the "terror of the Greeks" ("Terror Graecorum"), raided with his ships Methone that was used by pirates as a hideout.

Seventy years later, the Venetians enjoyed free trade in the "territory of Methone" and eventually claimed ownership of this area of the Peloponnese in the so-called "Partition Treaty" on the eve of the Fourth Crusade. A prominent figure of Methone during that period was

25. *Representation depicting a Venetian oared sailing vessel (galley).*

26. *The medieval fortified town of Methone, rendered by Konrad Grünemberg, in a manuscript of 1487.*

27

28

Nicholas of Methone, a significant ecclesiastical writer, active during the reign of Emperor Manuel I Komnenos (1143–1180), serving as his theological advisor and personal friend.

In 1207, Venetian galleys under Ranieri Dandolo and Ruggero Premarin seized the town of Methone rather easily, despite the resistance of the weak Frankish garrison. Without delay, they conquered Korone as well that had become a pirate haven.

In June 1209, Doge Pietro Ziani (1153–1230) (fig. 28) sent the new Venetian governor of Methone Raffaele Goro to the island of Sapientza where lay a significant Benedictine monastery, to resolve their territorial disputes with Geoffrey of Villehardouin (fig. 29), the first Frankish ruler of the Despotate of the Morea that had the castle of Kalamata as its capital (fig. 30). The Treaty of Sapientza (fig. 31) was signed on the homonymous island between Conon de Béthune, protobestiarios of the imperial court, and Guy d' Henruel, who represented the Latin emperor of Romania in Constantinople, Henri de Hainaut (known as Henry of Flanders) (1206–1216).

29

30

According to the treaty, the Venetians kept Methone with Sapientza as well as Korone and their administrative regions, whereas the Frank Geoffrey of Villehardouin remained ruler of Messene and the entire Peloponnese (fig. 29). Simultaneously, he swore an oath of perpetual fidelity to the Doge of Venice and his successors and undertook to send every year three gold-embroidered silk curtains, woven from the famous high-quality silk of Kalamata, two for Saint Mark's Basilica in Venice (fig. 34) and one for the Doge's palace.

The Venetians continued to hold Mothokorona (Methone and Korone) for about three centuries. The fortress of Methone in its present form is a creation of the Venetians (fig. 32). After 1210, when they occupied Crete, Methone served as a stronghold of their rich colony in the rivalry with the Genoese in the Aegean and the Adriatic Sea. Then settlers from various countries moved to Methone, and the small

27. Doge Domenico Michieli (1117–1130), also known as the "terror of the Greeks" (Terror Graecorum).

28. Doge Pietro Ziani (1153–1230).

29. Geoffrey of Villehardouin depicted on a French postage stamp.

30. The castle of the old town of Kalamata, a site identified with ancient Pharae

31. Map of Methone and Sapientza, where the homonymous treaty was signed in 1209.

promontory was fortified turning into a major port and anchorage for sailing vessels on their way to the coasts of the East.

Many Western chroniclers during that time referred to the entire Peloponnese as "L' île de Modon" or "Insula Montionis" (island of Methone). In his *Travelogue*, the German pilgrim Felix Faber reports that only in Methone one could find a ship for any place in the world. Owing to the development of trade, its population increased, whereas the great variety of ethnicities settled in the town (Jews, Greeks, Albanians, Venetians) gave rise to a multicultural society with its own laws.

Young female slaves, preferably of Tatar origin (fig. 33), aged between ten and twenty-four, were in high demand not just in Venice, the capital of the Most Serene Republic of Adria (fig. 34), but also in the two powerful Venetian castles of

Messenia. Notarial documents of the period between the 13th and the 16th century from Mothokorona pertain, among others, to slave trade between members of the upper middle class. Lorenzo Tommasao, a merchant from Methone, sold to Niccolò Montanari a twenty-year-old Tatar slave woman for twenty-five gold ducats. Also, a twenty-four-year-old slave woman,

named Dierormuo, was sold by Pietro Bon, a resident of Methone, for thirty-one gold ducats. This Tatar woman, although she was older than twenty, was sold at a relatively high price.

For around two hundred years, the twin colonies of Methone and Korone lived undisturbed by the Franks of the Despotate and the Greeks of Mystras. However, the Venetians suffered two crushing defeats in the sea off Methone: in 1295, when the Genoese destroyed the so-called "Caravan of Syria", and particularly in 1354, when the Genoese admiral Pagadino Doria, ancestor of the eminent Andrea Doria, captured in the naval battle of Sapientza the Venetian admiral Niccolò Pisani (1324–1380) with six hundred Venetian soldiers and thirty galleys which he sent to Genova as booty (fig. 35).

In the late 14th century, the Despot Theodore I Palaeologos engaged in an expansionist policy that was completed by his successors incorporating eventually the entire Frankish state. In 1394 the Venetians attempted in vain to unite the Greeks and the Franks against the Turks, whose incursions were getting closer; yet, the Greeks had different plans for the unification of the Morea.

32. View of Methone in a coloured drawing by Konrad Grünemberg, from a manuscript of 1490.

33. Slave market scene. In Venice, but also its fortresses in Messenia, young slave women were in high demand.

34. View of Sapientza, from the castle of Methone.

35. The medieval city of Genova, depicted in a coloured drawing.

The first half of the 15th century was a perilous time for the Venetian colonies in Messenia and Argolis because of the continuous raids launched by the Despot of Mystras (fig. 36) and the Turkish threat. In 1415, Emperor Manuel II, who had previously attempted to occupy the Greek possessions of Venice, asked the city to help in forming a common front of resistance of the Morea. Venice not only refused, but ordered the governors of Methone, Korone, Argos and Nauplia to deny entry into their territories to the emperor or his officers. In 1417, the castellans (*castellani*), namely the wardens of the castles of Methone and Korone, caused a rift between the Frank ruler of Achaea and the Byzantine despot of Mystras. Then war broke out, and during the forty years that followed, the despot's battalions swarmed the Morea that had been freed from the Franks, and at times plundered the borders of Messenia.

The Venetians retaliated by taking measures against the Greek population of the colonies. In 1444, the number of the Greek garrison troops of Methone decreased. The Greeks were prohibited from gathering together and establishing associations. Their property was confiscated and they were not allowed to own land. As a result, the Greeks migrated, the land was abandoned and the Venetians could not find people to cultivate it. When they decided to cut taxes in the hope of persuading their subjects to return, it was too late.

When the Despot Thomas Palaeologos, the brother of Constantine, the last emperor of Constantinople, fled by ship from Pylos to Venice, in 1460, and the last outpost of Eastern Rome fell, Sultan Mehmed II visited the Venetians in Messenia. He was well received and entertained, yet his troops plundered the country and killed many of its inhabitants. The Republic of Venice realized eventually the major menace and engaged in the reinforcement of the castle of Methone. In 1494, a traveller wrote on it:

"It is inhabited by 2,000 people, enclosed by the sea on both sides. It is well fortified and quite strong, yet flat ... The land is very fertile ... The dwellings are fine ... The walls abut onto the sea, and its harbour can accommodate large vessels. It has robust walls with a drawbridge in front of each of its four gates. It features many towers, and artillery weapons of all sizes are mounted on the towers and the walls. The part overlooking the mainland is very strong and continuously reinforced. The *Signoria* has added there a large moat and a double row of thick walls. It will be splendid once it is completed."

The Greeks, however, for fear of the Ottoman invasion, continued to migrate to other, safer regions under Venetian rule. In 1499 war broke out eventually. A Turkish ship was sunk in the Aegean as it failed to salute the Venetian flag; Sultan Bayezid II took revenge by dispatching a fleet of 250 vessels in order to attack the Venetian ports in Greece. Naupactus (fig. 37) was captured and Bayezid moved against Methone in 1500. Before the attack, all the houses outside the walls were set on fire and a barrier was built along the harbour allowing only one ship to pass through. The women were sent to Crete. The garrison numbered 7,000 men. For a whole month Bayezid laid siege to the castle by land deploying 100,000 infantrymen and 500 siege engines, whereas the Ottoman ships maintained a blockade.

The Venetian fleet, commanded by Melchior Trevisan, arrived and 27 of its galleys gave chase to 100 Ottoman vessels. Nevertheless, the Turkish ships returned when the Venetian galleys had been immobilized due to a dead calm, and the Venetians retreated with casualties, leaving the castle exposed. However, Trevisan reappeared with his fleet lined up for battle in order to enter the bay of Methone. On August 9 1500, four of his vessels filled with food, ammunition and reinforcements sailed to the mouth of the harbour, passing through a single line of Ottoman ships. At a fatal moment, the defenders abandoned the battlements to pull the chain that blocked the entry of Trevisan's ships into the harbour. The

36. The recently restored fortress town of Mystras, inscribed on the UNESCO World Heritage List since 1989.

Janissaries then penetrated the castle through the destroyed tower of the governor's palace and spread across the entire town, preventing the terrified inhabitants, who were running away, from burning down their houses and the ammunition so as not to fall into the clutches of the Ottomans. The Venetian garrison congregated in Bourtzi at the edge of the promontory in a last attempt to defend themselves. Those Venetians and Greeks who managed to escape, could see the flames of the burning castle from Zakynthos. The Turks killed all adults and enslaved all children under the age of twelve as well as the governor. They repaired the walls and installed at Methone families from various villages of the Peloponnese.

The Peloponnesian towns of Methone, Korone and Monemvasia constituted, as is known, significant trading centres and a strategic footing for the domination of Venice across the Levante. Therefore, the Most Serene Republic of Adria, based in Venice, that protected these ports by building strong fortresses, struggled to keep them as much as possible, although the rest of the Peloponnese had been captured by the Ottomans, almost in its entirety. Methone and Korone were eventually subjugated in 1500, and Monemvasia in 1540. The importance of the castle of Methone for the Venetians is made manifest in the *note verbale* of Doge Agostino Barbarigo delivered on September 7 1500 (one month after the colony's capture by the Ottomans) to the Pope, the king of Spain and other Western princes:

"We have lost the marvellous base for all ships sailing towards the East".

In 1531 the Knights Hospitaller from their stronghold in Rhodes attacked Turkish-occupied Methone. Initially, a group of Greeks advanced with two schooners and secretly entered the town having secured consent and the assistance of the Greek authorities of the port who were once subjects to the Order of Saint John. They occupied the tower of the pier and the entire town, covering the distance to the governor's palace at the north end. However, the rest of the Knights' navy delayed exposing themselves from their hiding place behind Sapientza island, and the rumour that the Ottoman relieving force was approaching, forced eventually the Knights to retreat after they pillaged the town of Methone and took one thousand six hundred men as captives, including the seven-year-old son of Aga, who later converted to Christianity and in 1555 was called the "Baptist of Methone".

In 1652 Methone was raided by Don Juan of Austria, following his victory at Lepanto (Naupactus). However, in Methone, as in Navarino Niokastro (fig. 38), the venture to liberate the castles and towns from the Ottoman rule failed.

Of particular interest is the ecclesiastical history of these three towns, as Venice had allowed Orthodox bishops to live side by side with their Catholic fellows, yet their presence in their main possession, Crete, was prohibited. Therefore, those from Crete who had to be ordained as priests could turn only to the Greek bishops of Methone or Korone, and later, when these towns fell, to the Bishop of Monemvasia. After the capture of Monemvasia in 1540, the ordination candidates travelled to Cythera, Cephalonia or elsewhere. The Bishoprics of Methone, Korone, Helos, Mani, Cythera, Rheoi (Prastos) and Zemena belonged to the Metropolis of Monemvasia, that was endowed with privileges granted by Byzantine emperors.

37. *General view of the castle and the harbour of Naupactus.*

In the last years of the 15th century, the episcopal throne of Methone was occupied by a significant scholar, the Cretan Ioannis Plousiadenos (1429–1500), a theologian, codicographer and fervent theoretical proponent of the Union proclaimed at Florence, who changed his name to Joseph. The ratification of Plousiadenos's election was found in the Venetian State Archives, dating August 28 1492, hence he must have been elected a year earlier, in 1491. The Venetian State ratified his election having recognized that he was "vir apprime catholicus et dominio nostro fidelissimus", namely "a predominantly Catholic man and most loyal to our authority". Methone's Catholic bishop at the time was Andrea Falco, who succeeded Ioannis (on December 12 1491) having been killed by the Ottomans during the capture of Methone in 1500. Following the ratification of his election, Plousiadenos settled in his See at Methone. In 1497 and 1498 he lived in Venice and at Christmas of 1498, he went to Rome. In the two years that followed, 1499 and 1500 (the last ones of his life), he was particularly active. In Venice he expressed his wish to visit his homeland, Crete, and the Doge presented him with a letter with kind words (dating June 25 1499), addressed to the Duke of Crete. This was the time when the Second Ottoman–Venetian War broke out (1499–1501) and shortly, in the first months of 1500, Methone suffered the first attacks by the Ottomans. Plousiadenos, despite his old age, rushed to Methone to fulfil his duty. Another letter from the Doge to the Duke of Crete, written four years after the events, on October 1 1504, refers to the valour Plousiadenos manifested during the siege of Methone, "encouraging, day and night, not just the civilians, but the fighters too". It remains unknown who his immediate successor was in Methone that was now under Ottoman rule.

38

SECOND VENETIAN RULE

On June 22 1686 the Venetians and the army of the Holy League landed at Methone. The Ottomans withdrew in the fortress, while the Venetians occupied the small "borgo", namely the lower town outside the moat, blocking the promontory by digging a perimetric entrenchment (circum-vallations) and building a series of breastworks in order to defend themselves from the arrival of the Serasker, the Turkish army commander, who was now accumulating his troops at Nisi (present-day Nea Messene). The Venetian Captain General Francesco Morosini (fig. 39) demanded the surrender of the fortress, reminding the Ottomans of Navarino and Korone, as examples of Venetian leniency but also revenge. The Dizdar, the Turkish garrison commander, replied that since men were born to die, he would defend the town to the death. Then the castle of Methone was bombarded by the Venetians who inflicted such damage and desolation that women and children were forced to lock themselves up in Bourtzi, the fortress on the islet at the south end of the promontory, where their voices could not be heard by the defenders of the rampart making them lose their courage.

Four days later, Morosini sent new envoys and the Ottomans asked to call a truce for one night. During that time, they engaged in the transfer of munitions to the battlements from an area that had been previously bombed, whereas in the meantime, the Venetians built new earthworks as far as the edge of the opposite side of the moat. The following day, the Disdar replied defiantly once more to Morosini who demanded

38. Aerial view of the Ottoman fortress of Niokastro. At its foot extends the present-day town of Pylos.

39, 40 The Venetian Captain General Francesco Morosini, Doge of Venice. Commemorative coin issued in 1688.

41. Palamidi at Nauplion was first fortified by the Venetians during the Second Venetian Rule.

42. View of the Venetian castle of Korone.

43. General view of the fortress town of Monemvasia.

the surrender of the Turks for a third time, as he was reluctant to destroy the fortress. The Ottomans, terrified by the delay and the anticipation of the Serasker's arrival, and mainly by the sight of the Venetians who hurriedly moved their siege engines inside the moat, ready to blow up the walls, hoisted eventually the white flag. On July 10 1686, four hundred Turks came out of the castle, leaving behind four hundred cannons and all the slaves, black and white, at the disposal of the Venetian administration and their dubious intentions of liberating them.

During the Second Venetian Rule (1686–1715), Methone became the capital of the Peloponnese district, while, from 1703 to 1715, it turned into the first seat of the Armenian Order of the Mekhitarists. This monastic order, which continues to maintain today significant spiritual establishments on the island of San Lazzaro in Venice, in Vienna and elsewhere, was founded in 1700 at Constantinople by Mekhitar of Sebasteia. In 1688, the Swedish general Köningsmark, who had played a key role in the conquest of Athens and the bombardment of the Parthenon, died at Methone.

The military campaign of the Ottomans to restore their rule over the Peloponnese, through combined operations on land and at sea, lasted seventy days, as the Vizier had sent an ultimatum first to the Venetian governor of Corinth, on June 29 1715, demanding his surrender. The resistance of the fortress, according to the official report by Captain General Daniel Dolfin to the Doge of Venice, lasted only five days. The Vizier split his army into two units, each consisting of 50,000 men. The first unit, commanded by himself, advanced to Nauplion, the capital of the kingdom of the Morea, whereas the second, led by the Serasker (Ottoman army commander) Kara Mustafa, moved against Patras, and other columns of the Ottoman army headed south. Nauplion (fig. 41) lasted nine more days. The Venetians evacuated Korone (fig. 42) and its small garrison joined its counterpart of Methone, which fought valiantly for three more days, but was ultimately forced to surrender on August 17 1715. On the 13th of the same month, the garrison of the castle of the Morea, namely of Rio, capitulated to the Serasker and, finally, on September 6, the Venetian commanders of Monemvasia (fig. 43), Ferigo Madoer and Vettor Lippomano, surrendered without resistance. Prior to that, they had put forth sixteen terms to the Kapudan Pasha (Grand Admiral) Hadji Mehmed, under which they would relinquish the fortress; most of these terms were accepted already the next day, on September 7. The Venetian garrison boarded the ships and departed undisturbed. However, according to published documents, the inhabitants endured suffering; they were all transferred to Constantinople as captives. Hence, the campaign for the recapture of the Peloponnese commenced on June 29 1715 and ended on September of the same year. The army of the Grand Vizier Ali numbered 100,000 men, whereas the Venetian forces consisted of just 4,527 soldiers arranged as follows: Nauplion and Palamidi 1,747 (of which 397 were cavalrymen), Corinth 450, Monemvasia 279, Kelephas 43, Zarnata 68, Methone and Korone 719 (including 245 cavalrymen), Navarino 179 (including 125 cavalrymen) Achaea 466 (including 491 cavalrymen).

43

THE LIBERATION

The walls that had been seriously damaged during the siege of 1686 were repaired and enlarged by the Venetians with new structures on the side facing the land. In the 18th century they were left to rot and started to collapse. Colonel Willian Martin Leake, who visited Methone in 1805, describes the castle's preservation state:

"The condition of the walls is appalling, although, in terms of their construction, they are much more imposing than the ones of Niokastro. The front overlooking the land is considerably taller and features a moat that should have been filled with water communicating from sea to sea, yet now it is parched and full of debris. The towers and the walls towards the sea are deserted. Methone is a suitable and significant site that has always been inhabited; therefore, no remains of ancient Greek antiquity are found, as the ancient materials were used for the repair of the modern dwellings and fortifications".

The Ottoman garrison of Methone managed to withstand the siege laid by Greek and Russian forces commanded by Alexey Orlov in 1770, in which the bishop of Methone Anthimos Karakalos actively participated. On May 26 1770, Navarino, which had been occupied by the Russians on April 10 of the same year, was abandoned. Three years before the Orlov Revolt, the first Greek immigrants had departed from the harbour of Methone for the USA where they founded in Florida the city New Smyrna Beach.

The first —albeit failed— uprisings of the Greeks against the Ottoman rule, fomented by Catherine II of Russia (the first one in 1770, mainly in the Peloponnese, and the second,

from 1787 to 1792, organized by the Souliotes in Epirus) imparted the prominence of the Romantic spirit to the enslaved inhabitants of Greece and gave rise to the first manifestations of Philhellenism. As is natural, the Philhellenic movement reached its peak at the outbreak of the Greek War of Independence in 1821 and was marked by the strong presence of the English poet Byron (George Gordon Noel, 6th Baron Byron, 1788–1824) who participated in the Struggle and lost his life at Missolonghi in 1824 (figs. 45–46). Already with the publication of his poem *Childe Harold's Pilgrimage* in 1812, he succeeded in conveying the true image of modern Greece to the consciousness of Europeans.

Turkish-held Methone survived the siege of the Greeks in 1821, led by the bishop Gregorios and the Mothonian notables Nikolaos Georgakopoulos, Anagnostis Voutieridis and Eustathios Drakopoulos. Only Miaoulis managed, on April 30 1825, to set fire to twenty-eight Turkish ships anchored in Methone under the vice admiral of Egypt.

From 1825 to 1828, Methone served as an operation base of Ibrahim Pasha (1789–1848), who arrived in the town with 50 ships from which 5,000 Egyptian soldiers and 400 horses disembarked on the 11th and the 12th of February 1825. The tents of the Ottoman army were installed on the plain of Methone, while Ibrahim had settled in the old Turkish Government House inside the fortress. The deplorable living conditions of the Greek population, the massacres and the tortures, the horrific sight of the catastrophe, the slave market —not just of young women who were about to enter the harem and small children, but also of elderly women who

44. Greek fighter on horseback. Work by Nikos Nomikos.

45. The Exodus from Missolonghi. Drawing by a folk artist.

46. Portrait of Lord Byron dressed in gold-embroidered local costume. Work by Thomas Phillips, 1813 London, Government Art Collection

47. Ibrahim Pasha. Coloured lithograph by Maxim Gauci. Athens, Gennadius Library.

48. The expedition of Dramali (detail). Lithograph by Alexandros Isaias, 1839. Athens National Historical Museum.

49. "The slave market". Work by Paul Emil Jacobs, 1839. Private Collection.

50. Mavrokordatos defending Missolonghi. Drawing by Ludwig Michael von Schwanthaler (circa 1840), from the frieze of the Trophy Room, in King Otto's palace (now housing the Hellenic Parliament).

were intended for heavy work—, the desolation of the countryside and other sufferings of the population are described by a French scholar, who presents a rather grim picture in the significant book for the period titled *Deux années à Constantinople et en Morée 1825–1826* (*Two Years in Constantinople and the Morea 1825–1826*), published in London and Paris in 1828,

remaining anonymous as he signed with the initials C.D. (Charles Deval), using as his title the following description: "student translator of the king at Constantinople". C.D., after spending two years in Constantinople, embarked an English brig on a two-month journey visiting Smyrna, Lesbos, Chios, Crete and Navarino, ending in Methone, where he stayed for fifteen days. There, he was offered lodging in the residence of the Austrian consul Scassi, and visited on a daily basis the castle whose gates closed at six o'clock in the evening. Salaried French and Italian doctors and nurses, as well as the English physician of Lord Byron, who was taken prisoner at Missolonghi by Ibrahim Pasha himself when the Exodus took place, took care of the ailing of Ibrahim's army. The author visited Ibrahim and describes him as a "short, obese man with broad face. His nose is crooked, his eyes emit sparks, while cruelty was etched on his face". Nevertheless, the idealized portrait of the Turkish-Egyptian pasha that was published depicts a particularly charming young man, several years before his arrival in the Peloponnese in 1825 (fig. 47).

Ibrahim, as already mentioned, had installed his enormous headquarters in the old Turkish Government House of the fortress. At times, the large hall of the complex functioned as a theatre, at the request mainly of the French and the Italian doctors, where pantomimes and comedies were performed, accompanied by acrobatics, tightrope walking, dances and athletic games. On the large front curtain of the stage, a crescent moon was depicted crowned with laurel by a Victory. Behind the stage there was a gallery where women of the pasha's harem could watch the spectacle unnoticed. Female parts were played by young Greek men, who were frequently forced to perform the same role after the end of the act.

The arrival of the Egyptian troops under Ibrahim pasha in Methone in February 1825 and the threat of the recapture by the Ottomans of large part of the Peloponnese in the period from 1825 to 1828 provoked the interference of the Great Powers and the official Europe in the Greek affairs (figs. 48-50). On July 6 1827, the Treaty of London was signed between the governments of France, Great Britain and Russia who ordered

51. Heiden, Codrington and de Rigny, fleet commanders of the three Great Powers, who played a decisive role in the victory at the Naval Battle of Navarino.

52. The French commander-in-chief Maison, in a work of the early 19th century.

53. The Naval Battle of Navarino; oil painting by Ambroise Louis Garneray.

the commanders of their fleets in the Mediterranean to intercept supplies from Egypt to Ibrahim Pasha. The naval battle of Navarino, on October 10 1827, ended in the crushing defeat of the Turkish-Egyptian fleet (fig. 53). The fleet commanders of the three Great Powers were the French Henri de Rigny, the English Edward Codrington and the Russian Loggin Heiden (fig. 51).

A second Protocol, signed on July 7/19 1828 in London between the three Great Powers, stipulated the dispatch to the Peloponnese of a Corps of 14,000 men in three Divisions —under the commander-in-chief Maison (fig. 52) and the generals Sebastiani and Schneider—aiming at the complete evacuation of Ibrahim's troops from the region. Maison landed at Petalidi and camped temporarily in the marshy and unhealthy Gialova and later in Methone, while the other two generals encamped in Korone and Niokastro. The French troops were not allowed to advance towards Sterea Ellada so as to restore order there as well. The updated London Protocol (4/16 November 1828) prolonged the stay of part of the French expeditionary corps in the Morea for the restoration of the castles and the settlements of Methone, Korone and Niokastro.

Methone, like Niokastro, was eventually liberated in 1828 by the French commander-in-chief

53

Maison. Korone was surrendered directly to the Greeks. Its castle, therefore, did not undergo planned repairs; nor was its settlement urbanized by the engineers of the French expeditionary corps. Repairs and additions to the Methone castle took precedence, as it was in a better preservation state compared to the rest of the fortresses, according to a report by Maison, sent to the French Ministry of Armed Forces on October 11 1828. The renovation of the fortress as well as the intramural settlement of Methone (fig. 54) was undertaken by the French colonel Audoy who had designed and implemented the urban planning of the new city of Pylos built outside Niokastro.

The monumental north gateway of the Methone castle was renovated, while the wooden bridge was replaced by a stone-built structure that featured fourteen arches, 45m long and 4m high (fig. 54). Then the new town outside the fortress was built, based on the plans and under the supervision of the military engineering officer Joseph-Victor Audoy and the captain André Pierre-Bernard Dubard, approved and signed by the governor Kapodistrias (fig. 55). The new town of Methone became the seat of the French military headquarters and the Greek administration; therefore, it was repeatedly visited by Ioannis Kapodistrias. The Kapodistrian school of Methone was built during that time, being one of the first schools of the Greek state, also designed by Audoy. The French, among others, planted three hundred trees in the new town (planes, olives and poplars).

54

54. View of the castle of Methone. Aerial photograph from the northwest.

55. Ioannis Kapodistrias, Greece's first governor, at a young age.

56. The stone-built bridge with the fourteen arches at the castle of Methone (view from the west).

THE CASTLE OF METHONE

Many descriptions of Methone are found in old travel books, the most appealing of which are those by the Spanish Pedro Tafur (1436), who regarded its gardens as beautiful as those of Andalusia, the German Conrad Faber (1483), François-René Chateaubriand (1806), Charles Deval (1826) and the American Stephen Luce (1827–1917), according to whom at Methone one could actually gain more insight into the splendour of Venice than in Venice itself. There are also numerous copperplate engravings depicting Methone. The most beautiful of them were created in the 15th and the 16th century, but there are also later ones rendered by A. L. Castellan, Otto Magnus von Stackelberg (1810), and Prosper Baccuet (1829).

The French chevalier Benjamin Nicolas Marie Appert, who had dedicated his entire life to improving prison conditions, proposed, with the consent of King Otto, that a model prison be built inside the castle of Methone for all prisoners of Greece, men and women. In the end, he did not accomplish his purpose and decided to live the last years of his life (1855–1873) at

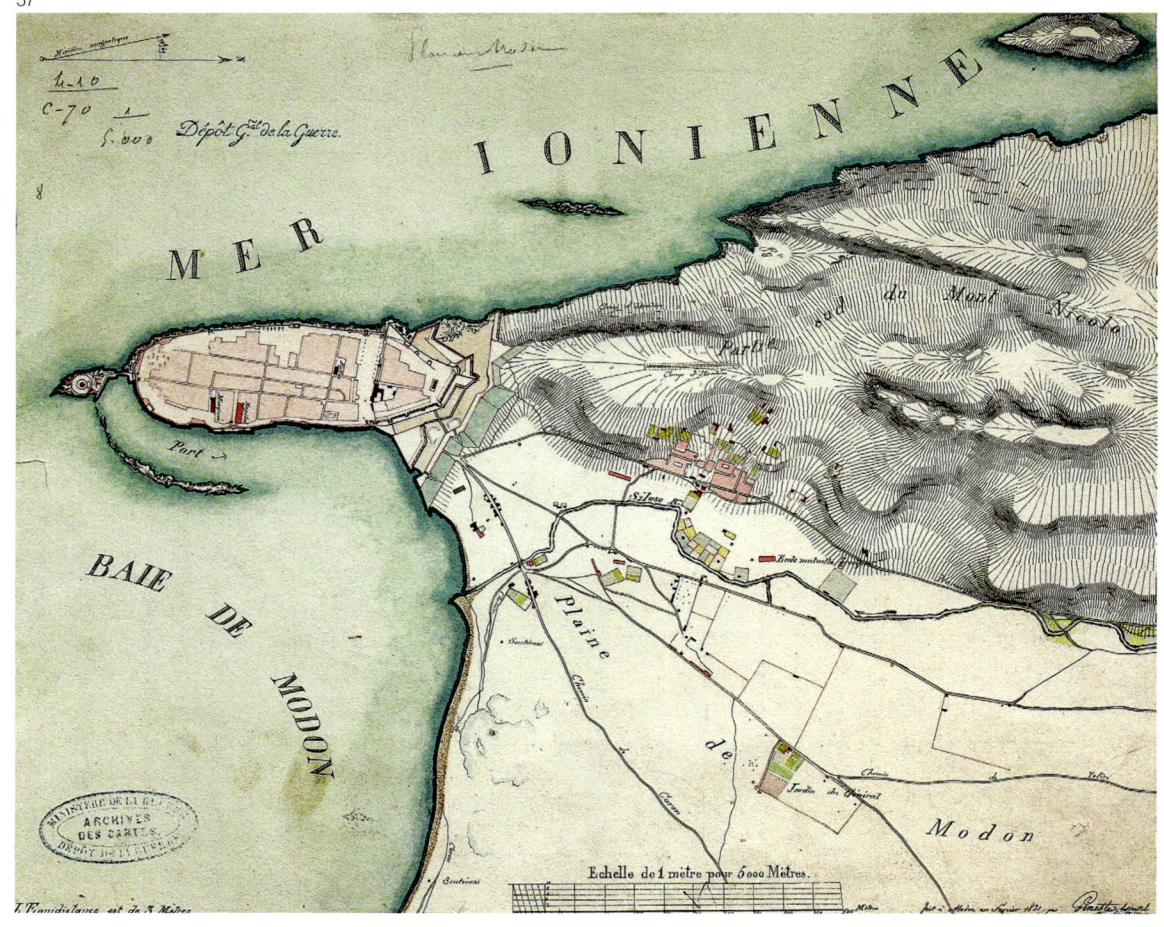

57

Methone alone and in poverty. In 1857 he rented all his belongings and his house to Nikolaos Torolopoulos for sixty drachmas per month. Marco Foscarini (1696–1763) in his book *Historia della Republica Veneta* (Venice 1722) describes the town of Methone as follows: *It is built on a promontory, stretching out into the sea, whose three sides are bathed in the sun* (fig. 57). *On the north side towards the mainland lies a fortress defending the front. It is furnished with a wide moat extending from sea to sea, of which the largest part is dug in the rock, built of stones on sloped terrain. The fortress is dominated by a section overlooking the town within the walls, the gate and the bridge. On the opposite end, where the enclosure protrudes into the sea, at a distance of around 30 paces from the walls, stands a small octagonal tower, widely known as the "lantern"* [he refers to Bourtzi] *that defends the canal* (fig. 58). *Controlled by the "lantern" beneath the east wall of the castle, there is a small harbour that in the past could take in 7 or 8 galleys, but now,*

57. Watercolour topographic map of the castle and the wider region of Methone (1831).

58. Aerial photograph of the castle of Methone as a promontory jutting out into the sea.

being deserted, it can hardly accommodate small boats. The enclosure is moderately high (without a platform for mounting cannons) with narrow square towers at intervals intended for decorative purposes rather than defence".

According to detailed descriptions of the castle of Methone, published by Greek and foreign researchers, the ellipsoidal promontory of Saint Nicholas, on which the castle is built takes the form of a cape projecting south into the sea, around four hundred metres long, covering an area of ninety-three thousand square metres. From the north-eastern corner of the promontory towards the east, the coast forms a deep curve, thus creating together with the island of Sapientza across the sea a large sheltered cove, which Venice first aspired to obtain for its merchant vessels.

The cape is enclosed by a fortification wall featuring relatively small towers at intervals that functioned as buttresses. The fortified space is divided into two sections with a cross-wall in between, reinforced with five towers. The north section was occupied by the old town of Methone, whose blocks, arranged within a pattern of streets and alleys, are still visible even today (see fig. 40). The northern part of the castle was specially reinforced with enormous and robust defensive structures built in order to effectively repel land invasions and serve as the governor's seat.

The castle is separated from the mainland, where the present-day settlement of Methone lies, by a large moat forming a wide arc along the neck of the promontory (fig. 59). The moat's escarpment supports on the south side a way

towards the castle, protected by tall walls (see fig. 60). On the west side of the moat, still visible are traces of a bulwark and the additions proposed by the *provveditori* (superintendents) Francesco Grimani and Agostino Sagredo. The escarp dates back to different time periods, as the Venetians during the last years of their second rule (1686–1715) changed the moat's direction so as to incorporate the prominent bastion built by Antonio Loredan in 1466 on the east coast. These renovations took place after 1701, when Grimani continued to serve as *Provveditore Generale delle Armi* (Superintended General of the Arms) (1698–1701). Since 1870, when the modern pier was built, the inner corner of the harbour was filled with sediment coming from the neighbouring torrent and the sea currents; as a result, the east walls of the castle as far as today's pier, against which the sea waves once lapped, now stand on a sandy shore.

On the east side, the moat's escarp stands on the sand running parallel to the front of the Antonio Loredan bastion for about 92m. Halfway, set into the moat's escarp, is a poros plaque depicting Saint Mark's lion carved in relief (fig. 61). Along the moat, up to the bridge, a barrel-vaulted passage in the thickness of the wall, namely a tunnel 1.80m high and 1.20m

59. Satellite photograph of the castle of Methone. Remains of a medieval jetty demarcating the harbour are visible on the seabed under the clear waters.

60. View (from the southeast) of the cross-wall that divides the castle of Methone into the north and the south section, where the citadel and the medieval settlement are found respectively.

wide, communicated with the moat through small entry points, built of large blocks of poros stone (fig. 62). Several other tunnels have been opened vertically to the interior of the main passage underneath the glacis, intended for underground explosions in case of siege.

At the north-western side of the stone bridge, there is a double ramp featuring large sloping steps. To the west, opposite the northernmost part of the castle, where a robust bastion forms a curve that turns into a straight line towards the west coast (fig. 63), the moat's escarp is vertical. On this side, it ends in a structure built shortly before 1715. It is a recessed rectangular level space —known today as "Heliodysion"— that protected this sector, in which the terrain, as it descends towards the coast, would otherwise reduce the effectiveness of the moat, leaving the north-western front of the castle exposed. On the side facing the sea, it is around 11m high; its lower half is built of ashlars and its base protrudes among the rugged rocks next to the water. Its north side is decorated with a plaque showing the lion of Venice, and a thick moulding along the top edge (fig. 64). Above, along the north side overlooking the heights of Saint Nicholas, the remains of a parapet with crenelations 4.50m deep are preserved. The other three sides also featured a parapet, 2.40m wide. The moat's widest point, between the Loredan and the Pietro Bembo bastions on the east and west respectively, is 39.50m wide.

Initially, the sea on the eastern side penetrated into the moat reaching a point just after the bridge. However, excavation to a greater depth of at least 6m would be required in order for the sea water to reach all the way to the west side. As colonel William Leake observed, this was the original intention of the Venetians when they commenced the undertaking in the late 15th century, but also when they decided to get back to it in the early 18th century. The work was suspended as a result of the capture of Methone by the Ottomans in 1715; however, following the naval battle of Navarino and the evacuation of Ibrahim's Turkish-Egyptian forces, the French troops of the commander-in chief Maison, in addition to their construction work in the town of Methone, continued to excavate and widen the moat. The moat is divided

61. Poros plaque with Saint Mark's lion in relief.

62. Semi-circular tunnel opening, built of poros blocks.

63. The northernmost part of the castle, where the robust bastion forms a curve that becomes a straight line towards the west coast, where the "Heliodysion" is found.

64. Bulwark in the centre of the large moat, bearing a plaque decorated with Saint Mark's lion in relief.

65

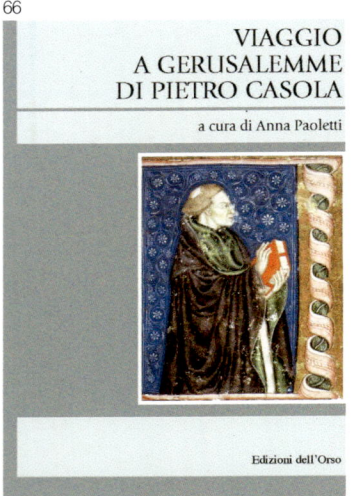
66

in the centre by a bulwark situated between the two furthermost polygonal towers (the Loredan and the Bembo bastions), creating a passage towards the original entrance to the castle beneath the west side of the Loredan bastion.

The main part of the moat dates back to the late 14th century, alongside the western Bembo bastion (fig. 65) the faussebraye (*falsabraga*) and the central section of the north escarpment as well as the glacis. The Loredan bastion, the lower terrace next to the east side of the Bembo bastion, the east section of the moat, and also the "Heliodysion" (artillery tower) at the west end of the moat feature the emblem of the winged lion of Venice and have been documented in the report of Agostino Sagredo on 1714 as recent additions to the castle.

The northern fortifications extend between the two large bastions and the artillery tower and include the double line of thick walls whose construction is referred to by the traveller Pietro Casola (1427–1507) that visited Methone in 1494 on his pilgrimage to Jerusalem (fig. 66). Their outer line rises 26m above the moat and is divided into two sections by an obtuse angle in the centre, while it also supports a roofed passageway that communicates with the two bastions. The west sloping section (escarp) is built of rough blocks of limestone, with firmly pointed joints upon which rests a low parapet. The south-eastern section is gently inclined, covered by thick reddish mortar, built of soft green sandstone, with two courses of poros stones that indicate the level of the roofed passageway. The parapet here is vertical and twice as tall as the parapet of the west section.

The castle has a total of six gates, three of which are found on the east side facing the harbour, while most of them open on the towers' ground-floor level, and are furnished with machicolations and portcullises high on the top part. The main entrance of the castle of Methone was originally situated in the centre of the south-eastern side of the large moat, and access was gained by crossing the moat and entering through an opening in the bulwark, namely the faussebraye (*falsabraga*) mentioned above. Today, very few remains

of the original entrance are preserved, which fell into disuse when the tall parapet was built and a new entry point was constructed by the French —at the end of the Greek War of Independence, from 1828 to 1830—, who also built the stone bridge with the fourteen arches leading to the main gate above the moat. This northern gate towards the land was reinforced for improved defence, in conformity with the rules of advanced fortification techniques, also aiming to withstand the power of cannons (fig.

65. View of the western Bembo bastion.

66. Front cover of a publication on Pietro Casola's pilgrimage to Jerusalem.

67. The arched bridge of 1828 leading to the castle's main entrance.

68. Detail of the relief decorative elements of the main gateway, depicting medieval weapons.
Photo: Panagiotis Foutakis.

67). The gate's front around the arched opening is indeed impressive, as it is built of finely dressed rectangular blocks of stone and is embellished on either side of the opening with two pseudo-pilasters crowned with Corinthian pilaster-capitals, and also with decorative elements diagonally arranged, accentuating its Renaissance character (figs. 68–69).

After the main gate, follows a narrow corridor, partly barrel-vaulted, interrupted by successive entry points (figs. 70–72). It terminates, through the cross-wall with the arched opening (fig. 73), in a wide central platform situated between the north and the south section, known as the "Great Terreplein", the centre of the financial and social life of Methone's inhabitants (fig. 75). The terreplein is dominated by an imposing unfluted column made of reddish granite, the so-called "column of Morosini", surmounted by

69. Two relief plaques set into a wall, depicting Saint Mark's winged lions.

70–72. The narrow corridor through which access to the castle is gained, with two successive doorways.

73. The outer gate of the narrow entrance corridor ending in the Great Terreplein.

70

72

71

73

74. The so-called "column of Morosini" made of granite, crowned with a Venetian capital of 1493, predating Morosini's arrival at Methone.

75. The Great Terreplein, during inspection of the Bavarian army. Watercolour by Hans Hanke (1834).

76. General view of the cross-wall separating the citadel from the lower town on the south. The Great Terreplein dominates the foreground.

77. The holy church of the Transfiguration of the Saviour, after restoration.

78. The gunpowder magazine covered with pavilion roof.

a capital of the first Venetian rule dating back to 1493 (fig. 74). This granite column comes possibly from a Roman building, as is the case with the colossal granite columns of the Roman proscenium of the theatre of ancient Messene.

Centrally located in the spacious terreplein, is the church of the Transfiguration of the Saviour (fig. 77), a timber-roofed, aisleless church built during the Second Venetian Rule. At a relatively short distance, to the west of the terreplein and almost immediately adjacent to the west wall, stands a small rectangular structure featuring pavilion roof (fig. 78) that functioned as a gunpowder magazine during the early years of the Ottoman Occupation and the Second Venetian Rule.

The north side of the Great Terreplein is demarcated by the cross-wall and its five towers, one of which has a gate on ground-floor level that

79, 81. The Ottoman gate to the castle's citadel.

80. The Ottoman baths (hammam) in the settlement of the castle.

79. Remains of the minaret of an Ottoman mosque.

83–84. Remains of the towers with the eastern gates facing the harbour. View of the castle's bailey.

constitutes a typical example of the period of the Turkish Occupation and leads to the highest part of the citadel (figs. 79, 81). In this section of the tower with the gate lay the multi-storeyed residence and the harem of Ibrahim Pasha —where theatrical performances also took place—, which later served as the abode of the French commander-in-chief Maison (fig. 75). Along the main street (*mercado publico*) heading south, from the Great Terreplein towards Bourtzi, are found the architectural remains of two Ottoman baths (*hammam*) dating back to the period of the first Ottoman Occupation (fig. 81). The best preserved northern *hammam* consists of vaulted chambers, with functions similar to those of the Roman baths heated by a hypocaust system, and included an *apodyterium* (changing room), a *tepidarium* (for lukewarm baths), a *caldarium* (for hot baths) and a pool (*piscina*). Near the southern *hammam*, the scant remains of the Orthodox church of Saint John the Theologian survive, which was converted into a Catholic cathedral and later into an Ottoman mosque, of which only the base and the lower part of a minaret are preserved (fig. 82). Streets perpendicular to the main thoroughfare, heading towards Bourtzi, lead to two gate-towers of the eastern wall, associated with the activities of the harbour: the Porta Stoppa and the Porta del Mandrachio (figs. 83–84). Unfortunately, the largest part of the top section of these gate-towers collapsed in the 1940s. Only one photograph taken in 1832 is preserved in the Archives of the Association of Friends of Methone's Castle that depicts the Porta del Mandrachio before the devastation (fig. 89) (the photograph is published with kind permission of the aforementioned Association).

85–88. Views of the magnificent south-eastern tower, after its restoration, with the twin passageways that feature pointed barrel-vaults.

89. The tower with the eastern Porta del Mandrachio facing the sea at the harbour, in a photograph of 1832.

90. Partial view of the south-eastern tower from the west.

Among the most impressive remains of the fortress complex dating from the First Venetian Rule of Methone is the south-eastern tower (figs. 85–88), situated between the east Porta dell Mandrachio and the south seaward Porta di San Marco discussed below. Some researchers have identified the south-eastern tower in a gravure of 1483 rendered by Eberhard Reuwich. This tower consists of two spaces resting on horizontal structures, built of finely worked masonry, featuring openings with tall, pointed barrel-vaults set into ornate frames made of carved poros stone blocks, that run parallel to corridors at a great depth, communicating with each other but also with the rampart-walk of the east walls (figs. 87–88). A low pointed doorway is found at the north side of the tower, whereas on the side facing the sea, there was no gate, apart from two arched windows arranged at the same height as the battlements (fig. 90). A stone-built stairway preserved in the tower's interior indicates that there was a second storey above the spaces with the pointed arches that have now been restored.

At the south end of the fortress stands the restored Gate of the Sea, the so-called Porta di San Marco, with an arched entry point on ground-floor level, flanked by two tall rectangular twin towers with battlements and an impressively large arched span between them on the top part (fig. 91). The gate leads through a built footbridge to Bourtzi, the seaward fortress that occupies a rocky islet, identified by some researchers as the "rock Mothon" mentioned by Pausanias (figs. 92–94). Bourtzi consists of an octagonal tower with battlements, enclosed by an octagonal wall that also features battlements

89

90

and a gate. A second domed octagonal tower, smaller in size, rests on the lower structure which is much wider. Inside the main space of the lower tower lies a rectangular cistern. A ramp leads to the rampart-walk of the circuit wall and from there to the main space of the second tall tower that contains embrasures around its circumference. The main space of the lofty tower consisted initially of four storeys with wooden floors, of which only the rafter sockets are preserved around the wall. The construction of Bourtzi commenced in 1500 by the Venetians, but was completed in the 16th century by the Ottomans, and was used at times as a garrison tower, a lighthouse, a prison, a shelter for civilians, but also a temporary storage facility for antiquities.

The west seaward wall of the Methone castle, extending around four hundred metres in total length, features upright walls, reaching the battlements, and six towers arranged at intervals (fig. 95). Similar to the entire enclosure wall, its masonry consists of compact rubble infill set in lime mortar as binding agent, faced with finely pointed dressed blocks of stone (fig. 97). Its foundations undergo gradual erosion due to the structure's direct exposure to north-westerly winds that sometimes become stormy and the sea waves, therefore, instances of collapse are not infrequent. (fig. 96). Bombardment during

91

92

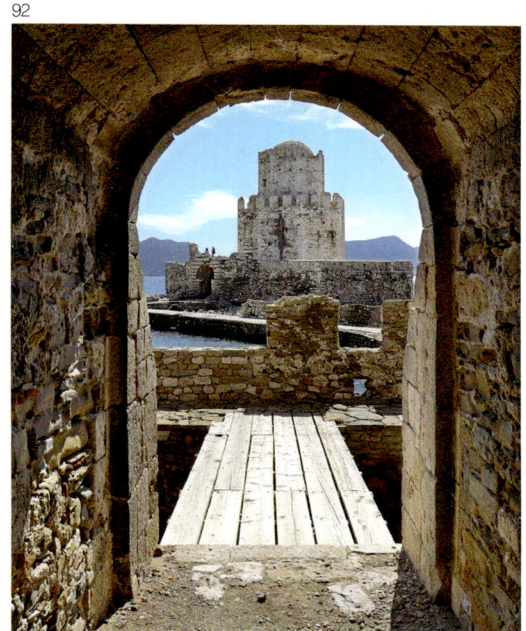

91. The imposing southern Sea Gate (Porta di San Marco), with the so-called "royal terrace" (view from the south).

92–94. The octagonal seaward fortress, known as Bourtzi, at the southernmost end of the castle of Methone. Photo 93 by Panagiotis Foutakis.

94

93

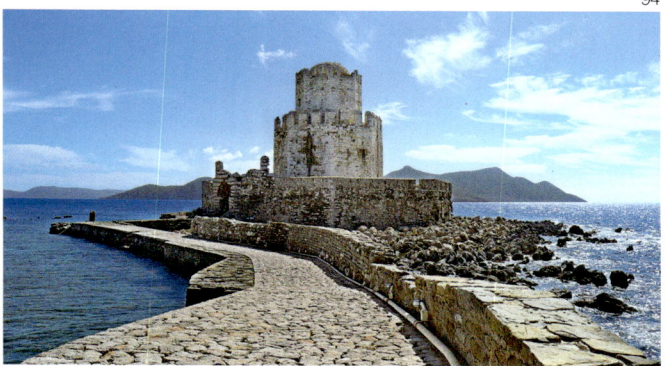

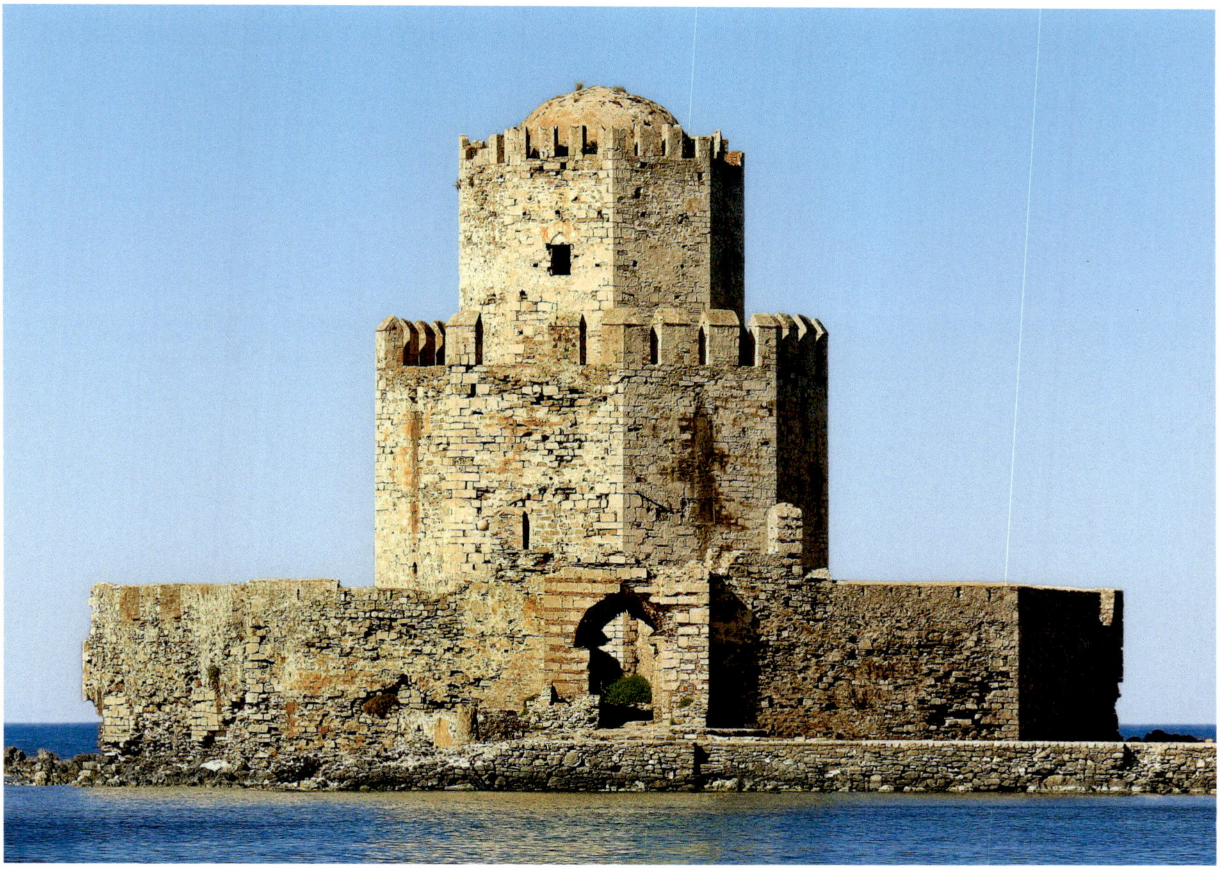

World War II has created gaping craters in at least four sections of the west wall that nonetheless, are gradually being brought back to their original form on account of the consolidation and restoration work undertaken by the Ephorate of Antiquities of Messenia.

95. General view of the east side of the castle of Methone. Photo by Panagiotis Foutakis.

96. Detail showing the collapse of part of the wall of the west side.

97. Fortification masonry technique that involves rubble as core infill. Photo by Panagiotis Foutakis.

MODERN METHONE

As already mentioned, after 1828, the liberating troops of the French commander-in-chief Maison engaged in the construction of the new town of Methone, outside the walls (fig. 98), using as building material stone blocks that belonged to intramural dwellings, as was the case with Niokastro and the new town of Pylos. In 1830, the single-nave church of the Transfiguration of the Saviour underwent consolidation.

In 1833, in the reign of King Otto, Methone became the capital of the homonymous district, renamed in 1836 district of Pylia. In Kapodistrias's governorship, a Cretan settlement was established that became a municipality. Cretan

98

refugees settled in Methone once again in 1866, but also people from Zakynthos, Lefkada, Paros, Arcadia, Patras, Argos and Chios, who were given national land and were introduced to potato cultivation. Today, in Methone one can still find descendants of Turks, Jews and other ethnicities, many of whom had served in the French Army under the commander-in-chief Maison, such as Italians and Arabs. During that time, the first

98. Aerial view of the modern town of Methone, stretching outside the medieval fortress.

carriageway was planned and paved, twelve kilometres long, between Pylos and Methone, while a second carriageway connected Argos with Nauplion.

From 1863 to his death in 1873 lived in Methone, as already mentioned, the chevalier Benjamin Nicolas Marie Appert —a friend of Balzac and a source of inspiration for Stendhal—, who fought in vain to realize his vision, the establishment of a model prison inside the Methone castle. In 1883 Konstantinos Romaios, distinguished professor of Archaeology at the University of Thessalonike and folklorist, from Vourvoura in Laconia, arrived in Methone at the age of nine, alongside his father who was teaching at that time at the Kapodistrian school.

During World War II, in anticipation of the allied invasion, the castle of Methone was reinforced by the Italians, through a range of defensive works along the coast. The Germans had set up to the east of Methone a large radiotelegraphy station, recording the English airplanes in the summer of 1944. In December 1941, at Methone, the Italian ship "Sebastiano Veniero" that carried 3,000 English, Australian, New Zealander and other war prisoners, was torpedoed by an English submarine and was destroyed as it crashed into the rocks. The corroded carcass of a crane from the Italian shipwreck lies derelict at the north-western end of the castle (fig. 101).

The splendour of medieval Methone has now been lost for good; today the small town, with a population of 1,200 souls, flourishes owing to the tourism industry, as it abuts onto the walls of its old, yet still proud castle that encloses material remains thousands of years old, battered by the sea. The four large wells of the town, created during the Second Venetian Rule (1686–1715) have been designated as historic monuments, whereas in 1985 the entire castle was declared, by the Ministerial Decision ΥΠΠΟ/ΑΡΧ/Β1/Φ30/3715/84/15-2-1985, a prominent Byzantine monument. The Kapodistrian school functions today as a cultural centre, following its restoration in 2015 (figs. 99–100).

BIBLIOGRAPHY

Andrews, K., *Castles of the Morea*, Amsterdam 1978.

Beis, N. A., Modon, *Encyclopaedia of Islam* III (Leiden, London, 1936).

Biris, Y., *Ένας δρόμος στο νότο: Χώρα, Πύλος, Μεθώνη. Το βασίλειο του Νέστορα*, Athens 1993.

Blouert, A., *Expédition scientifique de Morée, Architecture* I, Paris 1831.

Bon, A., *La Péloponnèse Byzantin jusqu'en 1204*, Paris 1951.

Bourazeli E., *Ο βίος του Ελληνικού λαού κατά την Τουρκοκρατίαν επί τη βάσει των ξένων περιηγητών* I, Athens 1939.

Breydebach, v. B., *Peregrinationes in Terram Sanctam*, Mainz 1486.

Demodos, T., *Ιστορικά και λογοτεχνικά κείμενα, Μεθώνη, Ναυαρίνο, Κορώνη* (selection – editing: O. Tsekouras and A. Tsirgos), Σύλλογος Φίλων Κάστρου Μεθώνης 2019.

Doukakis, D. Chr., Επισκοπή Μεθώνης, *Εκκλησιαστικός Φάρος* 6 (1910), 24–42.

Foutakis, P., *Η Μεθώνη και η Ιστορία, η Βενετία και η εξουσία*, Athens 2017.

Gell, N., *Itinerary of the Morea*, London 1817.

Kalogerakou, P. P., Η συμβολή του γαλλικού εκστρατευτικού σώματος στην αποκατάσταση των φρουρίων και των πόλεων της Μεσσηνίας (thesis), 2010.

Karpodini-Dmimtriadi, E., *Κάστρα της Πελοποννήσου*, Athens 1980.

Kotsiris, N., *Συμβολή στην ιστορία της Μεθώνης*, Athens ²1983.

Lambros, S., Έγγραφα σχετικά με τη Μεθώνη και τις άλλες κτήσεις της Βεν. Δημοκρατίας στην Πελοπόννησο, *Ιστορικά Μελετήματα*, Athens 1884, 173–200.

Leake, W. M., *Travels in the Morea* I–III, London 1830.

Loukos, Ch., *Η αντιπολίτευση κατά του Κυβερνήτη Ιω. Καποδίστρια 1828–1831*, Athens 1988.

Manousakas, M. I., Αρχιερείς Μεθώνης, Κορώνης και Μονεμβασίας, *Πελοποννησιακά Γ΄–Δ΄* (1958–1959), Athens 1960, 95–100.

Mertzios, K. D., Πότε και πώς έπεσεν η Μάνη εις χείρας των Τούρκων, *Πελοποννησιακά Γ΄–Δ΄* (1958–1959), Athens 1960, 277.

Miller, W., *Ιστορία της Φραγκοκρατίας εν Ελλάδι (1204–1566)*, trans. S. P. Lambrou, with additions and amendments, vol. II, Athens, 1909–1910.

Momferatos, A., *Μεθώνη και Κορώνη επί Ενετοκρατίας*, Athens 1914.

Pallas, D., Μεσαιωνικά Μεσσηνίας, Μεθώνη, *ΑΔ* 17 (1961–1962), Χρονικά, 103–105.

Soulis, G. C., Notes on Venetian Modon, *Πελοποννησιακά Γ΄–Δ΄* (1958–1959), Athens 1960, 267–275.

Zakythinos, D. A., *Le despotat grec de Morée* 2, Athens 1953.

99–100. The Kapodistrian school, restored by the Ephorate of Antiquities of Messenia, that functions today as a cultural centre.

101. Part of a crane from the Italian ship "Sebastiano Veniero" wrecked in 1941.

102. The sarcophagi shipwreck. They date back to the 2nd c. AD and come from Assos in Asia Minor. The ship that transferred them to Rome sank in the sea off Methone.

103. The main group of monolithic columns of reddish granite in the shipwreck of the Methone cove. They come from Tyre and Baalbek in Lebanon. Following the siege, capture and pillage of Tyre in 1124, the fleet of Doge Domenico Michieli departed for Venice. In the spring of 1125, it made a stop at Methone and one of its ships sank in its cove.

The granite column, the so-called "column of Morosini", in the Great Terreplein, comes from this shipwreck.

SOURCES OF ILLUSTRATIONS

ARCHIVES: Shutterstock: pp. 1, 4 • Kapon Editions: p. 5, figs. 5, 6, 14, 20, 21, 56, 65, 67, 69, 70, 71, 72, 73, 74, 76, 78, 79, 80, 81, 82, 83, 84, 85, 86, 87, 88, 90, 91, 92. 94 • Author's: figs. 1, 2, 3, 4, 7, 8, 9, 10, 11, 12, 13, 15, 16, 22, 23, 24, 25, 27, 28, 29, 30, 31, 33, 34, 35, 36, 37, 38, 39, 40, 41, 42, 43, 45, 51, 52, 54, 58, 60, 61, 62, 63, 64, 66, 77, 89, 96, 98, 99, 100, 101 • Panagiotis Foutakis: cover, figs. 17, 18, 19, 68, 93, 95, 97, 102, 103

BOOKS: P. Foutakis, *Η Μεθώνη και η ιστορία - η Βενετία και η εξουσία,* Kapon Editions, Athens 2017: figs. 26, 32, 57, 59 • A. Kakouri, *Αλφαβητάρι Νεοελληνικής Ιστορίας. Επανάσταση - Καποδίστριας - Όθων. 1821-1862,* Kapon Editions, Athens 2021: figs. 44, 46, 47, 49, 53, 55 • M. Momferatou, *Το καλογεράκι του Μυστρά,* Kapon Editions, Athens 2021: figs. 48, 50 • A. Papageorgiou-Venetas, *Ernst Curtius. Το ταξίδι του Νόστου στην Ελλάδα 1837-1840*, Kapon Editions, Athens 2019: fig. 75

CREATIVE DIRECTOR: MOSES KAPON
ARTISTIC DESIGNER: RACHEL MISDRAHI-KAPON
TEXT EDITING: DIMITRIOS DOUMAS
DTP: ELENI VALMA, MINA MANTA, EVGENIA STASSINAKI
PROCESSING OF ILLUSTRATIONS: MICHALIS TZANNETAKIS